Instruction Book

No. 8148

The Edison

Three-wire System

GENERAL ELECTRIC COMPANY

SCHENECTADY, N. Y.

DEC. 19, 1900

GREAT
THAT
IS
BRINGETH
THE
GIFT
KNOWLEDGE
NON EST
MORTVVS
QVI
SCIENTIAM
VIVIFICAVIT
THE JOHN CRERAR
LIBRARY CHICAGO.
1894
PRESENTED BY

Instruction Book

No. 8148

The Edison
Three-wire System

GENERAL ELECTRIC COMPANY

SCHENECTADY, N. Y.

DEC. 19, 1900

THE EDISON THREE-WIRE SYSTEM.

The general principles of the Edison Three-wire System are very simple, involving only the connection of two generators in series and the carrying of a tap from the connection between them, thus providing three wires for the transmission of current from the two generators.

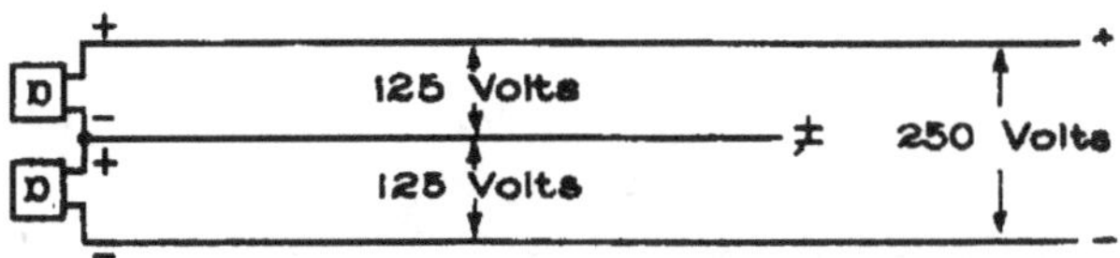

The outside wires are respectively positive (+) and negative (—) and the middle wire is called the neutral (±). When there is an exact balance of incandescent lamps or other load on each side of the system, there will be no current in the neutral wire. An excess of load on the positive side will produce an incoming current in the neutral and an excess of load on the negative side will produce an outgoing current in the neutral. The current in the neutral wire is in both cases a measure of the difference in the load between the two sides of the system.

The capacity of the plant may be increased by adding any even number of dynamos of the same voltage as the first pair, and connecting them in the same manner to the respective conductors, thus:

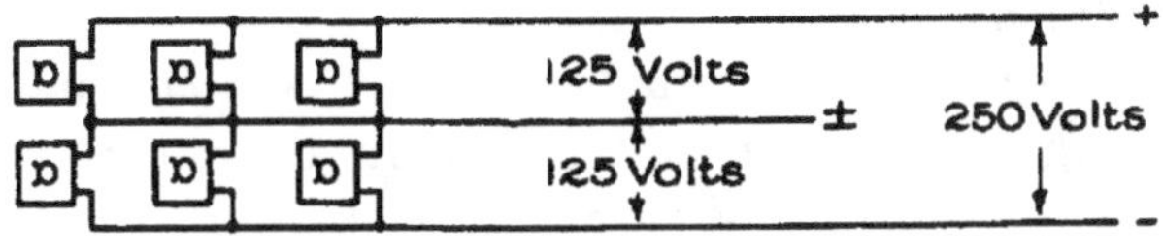

The capacity may also be increased by the addition of single dynamos that generate current at double the voltage of the above mentioned units, and connecting these generators directly between the positive and negative conductors, thus:

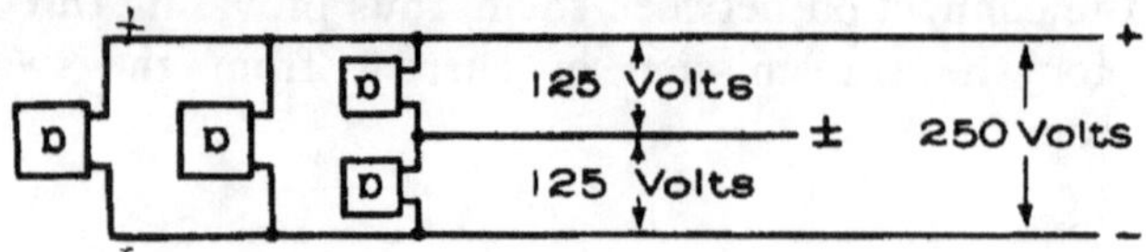

Storage batteries may also be used in conjunction with generators, to help out at times of heavy load.

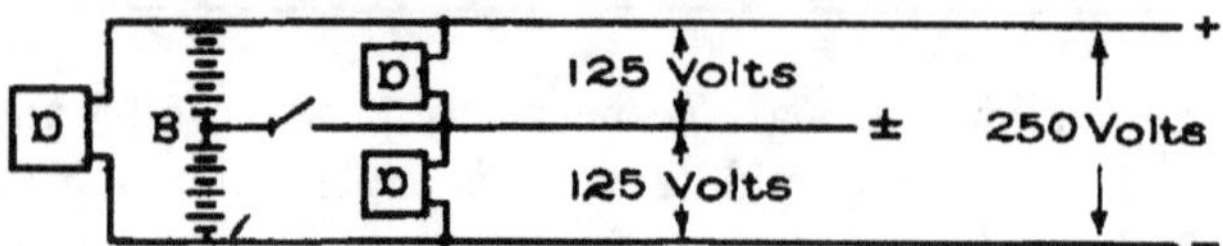

It will be seen from the above sketch that the storage battery can be made to balance the system, by connecting the two middle cells through a switch to the neutral wire. It is not generally advisable to use a battery alone and continuously for balancing purposes, as an unbalanced condition of load would necessarily work one side of the battery harder than the other. A storage battery can be used to the best advantage when connected across the outside wires of the system, without any connection to the neutral, thus insuring an equal charge and discharge of all the cells. There is an advantage, however, in providing for a connection to neutral for use in case of necessity.

It is evident that many different combinations of generating units and batteries may be made to fit different conditions of local service, but sufficient capacity must always be connected to the neutral wire to take care of any possible unbalancing of load.

Single generating units of the proper voltage may also be connected between the two outside conductors and the balancing of the system may be effected by special apparatus.

NOMENCLATURE OF CONDUCTORS.

In this system the various conductors that are used outside of the generating station may be divided into six general classes, viz.:

1. Feeders.
2. Pressure Wires.
3. Mains.
4. Tie Lines.
5. Services.
6. House Wiring.

FEEDERS.

These conductors usually extend in unbroken lines from the station bus-bars to the various outside centers of distribution. They are generally composed of three wires or cables, which are respectively positive, negative and neutral. As the neutral conductor is required to carry only the unbalanced current of the circuit, it need not be so large as the positive or negative conductor. It is commonly made about one-third the sectional area. Thus, when the two outside conductors of the feeder have each a sectional area of 600,000 c.m., the neutral conductor should be 200,000 c.m. and the three conductors collectively would be called a No. 600 feeder.

Edison tubes were formerly used for underground feeders, but rubber or paper insulated cable is now generally employed. As feeders are continuous conductors, no taps are taken from them at any intermediate points between the two ends. Nearly all the faults that occur in underground conductors originate at the joints. It is therefore evident that a reduction in the number of joints must result in an improvement in the system.

INSULATION OF CABLE FEEDERS.

Rubber and paper are the two insulating materials commonly used for cable feeders, and each has its particular merits as an insulator under different conditions of service. Both rubber and paper insulated cables are usually protected by an outer sheathing of lead.

Paper insulation is cheaper than rubber and it will stand a higher working temperature without deterioration. It is therefore a safer insulator than rubber for cables that are liable to be overloaded. On the other hand, a paper covering retains its insulating properties only when free from moisture. Its usefulness is therefore entirely dependent on the integrity of the lead sheathing, and should this become punctured by electrolysis, mechanical injury, or any other cause, moisture will find a way through to the paper core, and destroy its insulating properties. Paper insulated cables are therefore frequently provided with an additional jacketing of prepared jute or tape over the lead sheathing, which serves as a mechanical protection.

Rubber insulation under usual conditions should be protected from mechanical injury by a lead sheathing. Being itself an excellent insulator and impervious to moisture, it may retain its insulating properties indefinitely, even when the lead sheathing has been partially destroyed. The soil in cities is, however, generally permeated with coal gas and other products which are liable to leak into the ducts and exercise a very destructive effect on unprotected rubber. It is therefore desirable in all cases to maintain the lead sheathing of the cables in the best possible condition, but in cables made with paper insulation the absolute continuity of the lead is indispensable.

The thickness of the lead sheathing will vary with the nature of the service, as well as with the size of the cable, but the following figures show the standard thicknesses for ordinary conditions, the diameters of the different cables being measured over the rubber or paper insulation:

DIAMETER OF CORE.	THICKNESS OF LEAD.	
	RUBBER CABLE.	PAPER CABLE.
Up to $\frac{7}{16}''$	$\frac{3}{64}''$	$\frac{1}{16}''$
$\frac{1}{2}''$ to $\frac{5}{8}''$	$\frac{1}{16}''$	$\frac{3}{32}''$
$\frac{11}{16}''$ to 1 $''$	$\frac{5}{64}''$	$\frac{7}{64}''$
$1\frac{1}{32}''$ to $1\frac{7}{16}''$	$\frac{3}{32}''$	$\frac{1}{8}''$
$1\frac{1}{2}''$ and larger.	$\frac{1}{8}''$	$\frac{1}{8}''$

The distance which cables can be drawn into ducts in a single length will depend on the diameter and weight of the cable, and the size and character of the duct, etc., but 300 to 500 ft. may be considered as a fair average distance, and it will seldom be found necessary or desirable to locate manholes any further apart than this.

It is common practice in European countries to use steel armored cable buried directly in the ground without any other protection. This cable is generally insulated with rubber, sheathed with lead, and wound with a jacket of prepared jute. It is then finally armored with two layers of steel ribbon wound on spirally and sometimes finished with another jacket of prepared jute.

A system using this kind of cable laid directly in trenches dug in the ground, is called a " built-in system," and its advantage over the "conduit" or "drawn-in system" is that almost any length of cable can be laid at one time in an open trench, thus avoiding all the trouble and expense of building ducts and drawing in the conductors. In fact, the length of an armored cable thus laid is governed more by the limitations of manufacturing and transportation than by the difficulties involved in the laying. This system has, however, the great disadvantage of being permanently buried, making repairs and additions difficult and costly. Steel armored cable has not found much favor in this country, our underground cables being almost universally unarmored, and drawn into conduits of wood, iron, or glazed stoneware.

When Edison tubes are used for feeders, they should be so laid that the positive conductor is on the right hand going away from the station, the negative being at the left hand and the neutral at the bottom. This rule should be invariably followed to facilitate connections and testing.

PRESSURE WIRES.

These wires are attached to the feeder ends at centers of distribution, and they extend back from thence to the station switchboard, where they are connected to volt indicators that show the electrical pressure at the feeder ends or points of distribution.

Three pressure wires are always incorporated in Edison tube feeders and it is also common practice to include pressure wires inside cable feeders, although some engineers prefer to have them made up separately. The latter method costs a little more than the combination, but it is more reliable, and therefore to be recommended. Separate pressure wire cables are usually made up with three No. 14 B. & S. wires separately insulated with rubber and enclosed in a common lead sheathing. When pressure wires are incorporated in feeder cables it is common practice to use No. 16 B. & S. rubber insulated wire and two of these are stranded in with the bare copper wires of the positive and negative cables, so that each feeder has four pressure wires, one of which may be used as a spare to operate any desired switching or signalling device. Particular care should be taken in drawing pressure wire cables into the ducts so that they may not be unduly strained or injured in any way, as these wires are vital parts of the system and their failure to operate properly is sure to entail considerable trouble and expense.

MAINS.

These conductors are connected to the feeders, at the points of distribution, and they branch out from thence in all directions through the district that is to be supplied with current.

Mains are usually interconnected at every convenient point so as to form a complete network of conductors. These cross connections greatly assist in equalizing the electrical pressure under changing conditions of load.

The house to house supply of current is taken from the mains and it therefore becomes necessary to connect branches or services to them as occasion demands. For this reason Edison tubes are generally used for mains in preference to cables. Main tubes are made with three conductors of equal size, as the neutral wire is often called upon to carry a considerable amount of balancing current between two different points of delivery. These tubes are laid in the ground with no other protection than a piece of 5″ x 2″ creosoted lumber laid over the top as a guard against accidental injury from picks, etc., and in many cases even this protection is omitted.

When it is desired to install tube mains along the route of cable feeders, the top of the feeder ducts should be covered with about six inches of sand and the tubes laid therein. In this case there should not be less than 18″ between the top of the tube and the street level, and 24″ is preferable. The six inches of sand will give good room for the round bottoms of the coupling boxes which extend a few inches below the bottom of the tubes.

In the absence of any conduit, tubes should be laid in trenches which are usually made about 30″ deep and 20″ wide at the bottom. Two tubes can be laid in a trench of these dimensions but it is not desirable to make the trench any narrower for one tube, as it is difficult to do good jointing in a cramped location.

In order to facilitate connecting and testing, the neutral conductor of tube mains should be located next to the curb of the sidewalk, with the positive at the top and the negative at the bottom.

TIE LINES.

Tie lines are usually large trunk conductors which are laid between different generating stations, for the purpose of transmitting current from one station to another, for the charging of storage batteries, the working of rotary converters, etc., or for the supply of current to a distant system when required.

Tie lines, being practically large feeders connecting two or more generating stations, are subject to the same general conditions as ordinary feeders and are usually composed of large rubber or paper insulated cables, pulled into ducts of glazed stoneware.

SERVICES.

These are short taps connecting the distributing mains with the customers' premises. They may be either two wire or three wire, according to the requirements of the customer or the rules of the local illuminating company. It is common practice in some large cities to supply small consumers, using 20 and sometimes as many as 40 16-candle-power lamps, through a two wire service, and larger consumers through a three wire service. It is, however, always best to run a three wire service into the premises of small customers, even if only two of the wires are used.

Underground services may be of either Edison tube or cable. For services of 100,000 c.m. and larger, tube is recommended, but three conductor cable run in ordinary iron pipes is generally used for smaller services.

ELECTRICAL LOSS IN CONDUCTORS.

The allowable electrical losses or drop of potential in the various parts of a distributing system under condition of maximum load must, of course, be governed by local considerations, such as prime cost of installation, cost of production, etc. In general practice, however, the following margins of loss are allowed:

Feeders, . . . 10% to 15%.
Mains, . . . 1% to 2%.
Tie Lines,. . . Variable.
Services, . . . ½% or less.
House Wiring, . . 2% to 3%.

EDISON TUBES AND FITTINGS.

As previously stated, the use of Edison tubes for feeders has been practically discontinued, so the following remarks will be understood as applying to main conductors.

Standard main tubes are made in twelve different sizes, each tube consisting of three solid copper conductors of equal size properly insulated within a wrought iron pipe.

TUBE NO.	SIZE OF EACH CONDUCTOR C.M.	WEIGHT LBS. PER FT.	SIZE OF IRON PIPE, INCHES.		MAX. CURRENT IN EACH OF TWO CONDUCTORS. AMPERES.
			Nominal Inside Diam.	Actual Outside Diam.	
41	41,000	3.75	$1\tfrac{1}{4}$	$1\tfrac{5}{8}$	100
80	80,000	4.3			200
100	100,000	4.5	$1\tfrac{1}{2}$	1.9	235
120	120,000	4.7			260
150	150,000	6.6			295
200	200,000	7.0	2	$2\tfrac{3}{8}$	350
250	250,000	7.4			400
300	300,000	7.8			450
350	350,000	11.0			495
400	400,000	11.4	$2\tfrac{1}{2}$	$2\tfrac{7}{8}$	540
450	450,000	11.8			580
500	500,000	12.3			620

Nos. 41 and 80 are seldom used excepting for services and are not recommended even for this purpose excepting under special conditions.

Larger sizes of Tubes for Feeders and Tie Lines are listed in regular catalogue.

The copper rods are all 20' 4" long and project from each end of the pipe. All 1½" and 2" pipes are cut 20' long, allowing copper rods to project 2" at each end. 2½" pipes are cut 19' 10" long, giving 3" projection of copper rods at each end. The rods are drawn of the finest and purest Lake copper having a conductivity of at least 98%. The wrought iron pipes are of the best grade of lap welded steam pipe, free from imperfections and of full weight. The tubes when connected measure 20' 6" from center to center of joints.

In making up a tube the ends of the copper rods are first chamfered and tinned, and the iron pipe is thoroughly cleaned on the inside. Two of the three copper rods are wound separately with spirals of prepared rope and the three rods are bound together with another spiral winding of rope. The bundle of rods is then slid into the iron pipe which has previously been warmed, and the pipe is filled with an insulating asphaltum compound by a special process which insures freedom from air bubbles. The ends of the pipe are closed with hard rubber plugs and the projecting ends of the copper rods are cleaned and otherwise prepared for the future operation of jointing. Finally the tubes are painted with japan and tested, and are then ready for shipment.

BOXES AND JOINTS USED FOR CONNECTING TUBES AND CABLES.

To meet the various requirements of underground electrical service, convenient devices have been designed for connecting tubes to each other in straight lines or at various angles, and also as branches at different angles from the main line.

STRAIGHT LINE JOINTS.

In coupling together two sections of Edison Main Tube, three flexible copper joints of uniform size are employed which are called "Straight Line Coupling Joints."

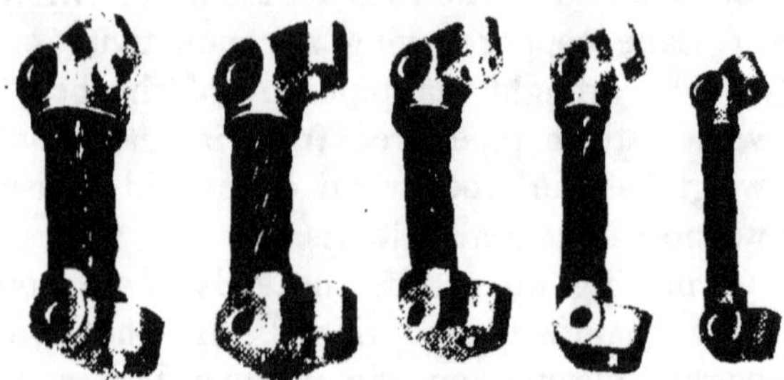

Fig. 1. STANDARD MAIN JOINTS.

There are two kinds of these joints, "Standard" and "Laminated." Standard joints are made by casting

Fig. 2. LAMINATED MAIN JOINTS.

composition sockets on the ends of short pieces of flexible copper cable, and laminated joints consist of a continuous length of thin flexible copper ribbon wound into a ring and formed into the required shape. Figs. 1 and 2 show different sizes of these two joints.

Standard joints are made for all sizes of conductors, but laminated joints are made only for sizes up to and including No. 250. All these joints have sockets that

Fig. 3. STRAIGHT LINE COUPLING BOX.

fit easily over the ends of the copper rods that they are intended to connect. After being put in place, they are soldered and the joint is enclosed in a cast iron box made in halves and called a "Straight Line Coupling Box," (Fig. 3) the two parts being fastened together by bolts on the flanges.

Fig. 4. BALL CLAMPS.

As it is difficult to place two lengths of tubing in exact alignment, "Ball Clamps" (Fig. 4) are bolted fast to the ends of the iron tubes. These ball clamps fit into sockets in the ends of the coupling boxes, forming a ball and socket joint, so that the two tubes can be laid, if necessary, as much as $12\frac{1}{2}°$ out of alignment in any direction. Fig. 5 illustrates the adaptation of the foregoing parts to a straight connection, showing only the lower half of the coupling box in place. When the

Fig. 5.

joints have been made, the top half of the coupling box is put on and bolted fast, and the box is filled with hot insulating compound, which surrounds and insulates the

Fig. 6.

ends of the copper rods, the joints, and the ends of the iron tubes.

This compound does not grow brittle on cooling, or with age, but remains plastic even at a very low temperature.

Fig. 3 illustrates a finished No. $2\frac{1}{2}$ straight line coupling box and Fig. 6 shows the top half of the same separate, with the round hole through which the melted compound is poured. This hole is closed with a cast iron cap which can be locked securely by giving it a quarter turn. The cap (Fig. 7) is called a "Ventilator Top," and it makes a dust-tight but not an air-tight joint.

Fig. 7.

VENTILATOR TOP.

Only three sizes of pipes are used for all conductors from No. 41 to No. 500 inclusive, so three sizes of coupling boxes are sufficient, and they are numbered in accordance with the largest size of pipe with which they can be used.

It is sometimes necessary to connect together two different sizes of tubes, as for instance, a No. 350 tube to a No. 200 tube, the latter being made in a 2″ pipe and the former in a 2½″ pipe.

In such cases "Ball Reducing Clamps" are required. At one end of the 2½″ coupling box a 2½″ x 2½″ ball clamp would be used for the 2½″ pipe, and at the other end a 2½″ x 2″ ball reducing clamp would secure the 2″ tube.

Ball reducing clamps are also made for connecting different sizes of tube to different sizes of triple conductor cable.

ANGLE OR ELBOW JOINTS.

When tubes are laid around corners or when their direction is otherwise diverted from a straight line to any considerable extent, special elbow boxes and joints are required.

Fig. 8 shows the arrangement of tubes and joints in a 90° elbow box. Several points of difference will be

Fig. 8.

noted between the internal fittings of this box and those of a straight line coupling box. In the latter the flexible joints are all of uniform length, but the shape of an elbow box requires the use of joints of different lengths.

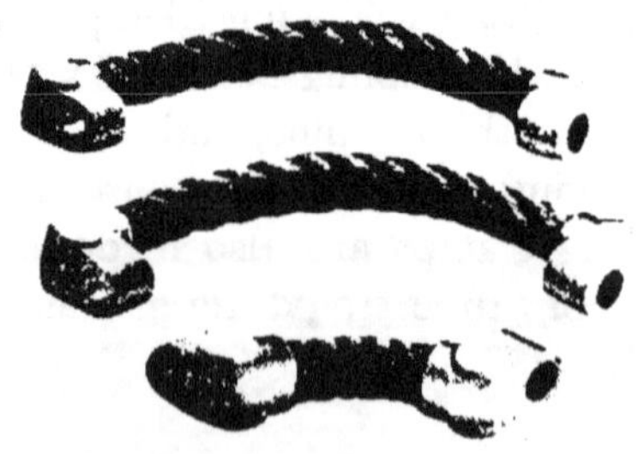

Fig. 9.

Fig. 9 illustrates a set of three elbow coupling joints, comprising one each, short, medium and long, and these joints are shown in position in Fig. 8.

It will also be seen that the clamps are of different form from those that are used with the straight line coupling boxes. Tubes that are connected together at different angles often require a wider range of movement from a mean position than tubes that are laid in a nominally straight line. Elbow coupling boxes are therefore fitted with Cup Clamps (Fig. 10) which are bolted to the ends of the iron tubes in the same way as Ball Clamps. They have spherical surfaces like ball clamps, but are constructed to give a range of about 20° in any direction from normal, whereas the ball clamps only permit a variation of $12\frac{1}{2}$°, as before stated.

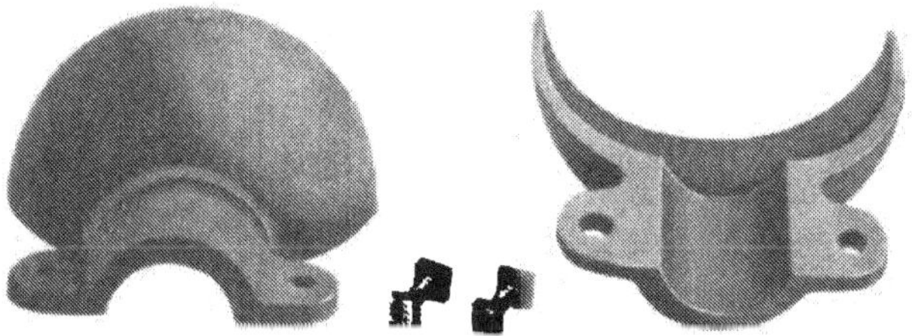

Fig. 10.
CUP CLAMPS.

Elbow boxes are made in three standard angles, 20°, 55° and 90°, so that with the range of movement permitted by the cup clamps, any desired angle can be given to the tubes up to 110°.

On account of the large angular variation permitted by cup clamps and often used in practice, elbow boxes must be of comparatively larger dimensions than straight line coupling boxes, as the copper joints are liable to spread out and ground against the cast iron wall of the box unless a good margin of space is allowed.

Thus 2″ straight line coupling boxes are all right for mains from No. 150 to No. 300 inclusive, as all these are included in 2″ pipes, but it is proper to use a 2½″ elbow box for the above sizes with a reducing clamp that will fit the 2″ pipe. The following table will further explain the required difference in sizes of boxes.

SIZES OF STRAIGHT LINE AND ELBOW COUPLING BOXES USED WITH DIFFERENT SIZES OF TUBES.

TUBE NO.	IRON PIPE.	STRAIGHT LINE COUPLING BOX.	ELBOW COUPLING BOX.
80 100 120	1½″	1½″	2 ″
150 200 250 300	2 ″	2 ″	2½″
350 400 450 500	2½″	2½″	3 ″

As previously explained under the heading of "Mains," it is customary to place main tubes so that the neutral conductor is next to the curb line, thus putting the other two conductors in a vertical position relative to each other, the upper one being made positive and the lower one negative.

Referring to Fig. 8, when an elbow box is turned towards the curb it is called an "inside" elbow and when it is turned towards the street it is called an "outside" elbow.

It will be seen that an "inside" elbow requires a short neutral joint, while an "outside" elbow requires a long neutral joint.

The following table will be found useful in ordering elbow joints.

JOINTS REQUIRED FOR "INSIDE" ELBOWS.

JOINTS.	ANGLE OF ELBOW BOX.		
	20°	55°	90°
Straight Line	1	—	—
Short . . .	—	1	1
Medium . .	2	2	—
Long . . .	—	—	2

JOINTS REQUIRED FOR "OUTSIDE" ELBOWS.

JOINTS.	20°	55°	90°
Straight Line	2	—	—
Short . . .	—	2	2
Medium . .	1	1	—
Long . . .	—	—	1

BRANCH CONNECTIONS.

One of the important advantages gained by using Edison Tubes instead of Cables for Mains is the facility with which branches or services can be connected to the main line for the house to house distribution of current. Main joints are drilled with additional holes at their ends for the connection of "Branch Coupling Joints," which are illustrated in Fig. 11. It will be seen that these joints have a socket at one end and a plain round stud or pin at the other end.

When connecting a service to a main, the pins of the joints are soldered into the holes in the main joints, and the ends of the service wires are soldered into the sockets. When Cable Services are laid, the ends may

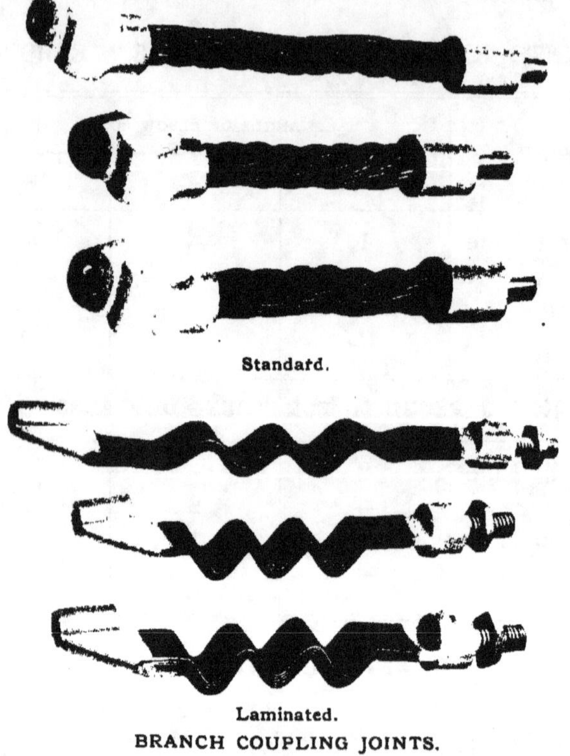

BRANCH COUPLING JOINTS.

Fig. 11.

sometimes be soldered directly into the side holes in the main joints, thus dispensing with any intermediate connections, but tube services always require the extra joints.

The Branch Coupling Box which is used to protect and insulate a service connection is similar to a Straight Line Coupling Box as far as the fittings to the main pipe are concerned, so that when putting in a service, the straight line box can be replaced by a branch coupling

Fig. 12.

box without disturbing the main connections or interrupting the electrical service. These boxes are

Fig. 13. "T" COUPLING BOX.

made in three forms, which are called, respectively, "T" Boxes, "Cross" Boxes, and "Y" Boxes.

A "Cross" box is simply a double "T" box, permitting two services to be taken from one joint.

A "Y" box is a modification of a "T" box and is used where a service is taken from the main line at an angle of 45°.   See Figs. 13 and 14.

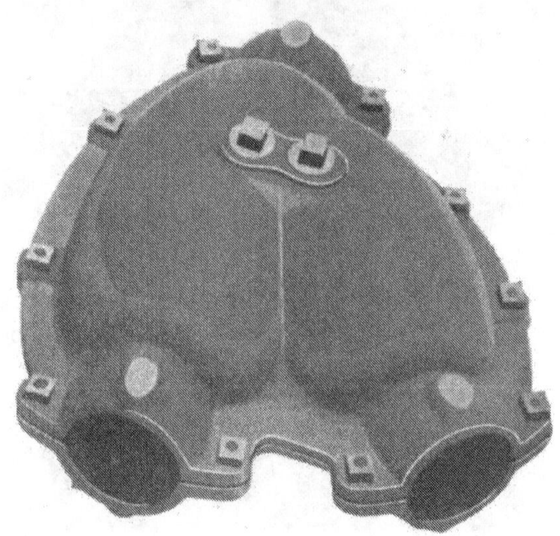

Fig. 14.

"Y" COUPLING BOX.

Branch connections, like elbow connections, are either "inside" or "outside," that is, if the branch or service connection is made towards the sidewalk it is called an "inside" service, but if it is made towards the street it is called an "outside" service.   The same boxes are used for inside and outside services, the change being made in the placing of the box.   The Branch Coupling Joints, however, differ with the direction of service, and these should be ordered from the following table:

SIZE OF MAIN.	BRANCH COUPLING JOINTS REQUIRED.
	FOR AN INSIDE SERVICE.
80 to 250	3 Short Branch Joints.
300 to 500	3 Long Branch Joints.
	FOR AN OUTSIDE SERVICE.
80 to 500	2 Short Branch Joints.
	1 Long Branch Joint.
	1 Branch Link.

Fig. 12 shows the lower half of a "T" box with an inside service connection.

Fig. 15.

COUPLING BOXES
WITH EXTENDED DOME COVERS.

Figs. 15 and 16 show coupling boxes, in which the top halves are enlarged in the shape of a deep bell or dome. This upward extension effectively prevents the

Fig. 16.

possibility of water creeping down to the joints through depressions or channels caused by the shrinking of the insulating compound when cooling. The enlargement, of course, calls for a little more compound than the ordinary standard box, but the small extra expense involved is considered by many to be more than justified by the additional safety insured.

WEIGHT OF COMPOUND REQUIRED FOR COUPLING BOXES.

The approximate weight (in pounds) of compound required for different boxes is given in the following table.

BOXES.	SIZES.			
	2"		2¼"	
	Stand.	Ex. Dome.	Stand.	Ex. Dome.
Straight Line Coupling Box	22	26	34	38
Elbow Boxes 90°	20	24	40	44
" " 55°	18	22	38	42
" " 20°	17	21	36	40
Cross Boxes	44	48	60	64
"T" "	28	32	49	53
"Y" "	28	32	49	53
End "	5		6	

NOTE. One cubic foot of compound weighs about 95 lbs., and one gallon weighs about 12 lbs.

END BOXES.

End boxes are designed to protect the ends of tubes from mechanical injury and moisture. They are used at the junction between a tube service and the cables leading to the house wiring, and also at the junction of tubes and cables in manholes.

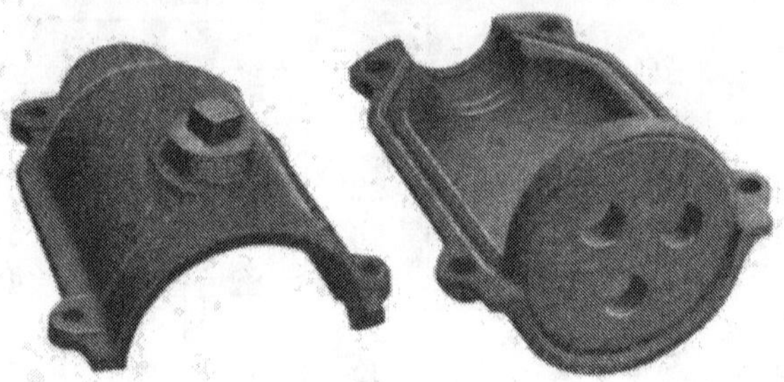

Fig. 17.

END BOX.

The blank end of the box is usually drilled with holes of the proper size to receive the cables and after the jointing is finished, the top half is bolted on and the box is filled with melted compound.

Services are sometimes installed before they are connected to the interior wiring. In such cases the end of the tube that projects into the cellar or basement should be always protected by an end box, the blank end of it being left solid.

GENERAL REMARKS ON LAYING AND JOINTING.

Trenches should be dug as nearly straight as possible avoiding all unnecessary bends, and corners should be square. Particular care should be taken to see that the tube has a solid and level bed to rest upon, and to insure this condition, a depression or pocket should be hollowed out under each coupling box, and the bottom of the trench between pockets should be carefully levelled. See Fig. 18.

Fig. 18.

When filling the trench use only fine dirt, free from stones, for covering the tubes and coupling boxes, under which the soil should be well tamped to insure a solid support for all portions of the line. After the tubes are well covered, heavy rammers should be used to thoroughly settle the dirt as it is shovelled into the ditch.

In cities where a great deal of excavating is done by different companies and individuals, it is a good plan to place 5″ x 2″ planks of creosoted pine over the tubes to protect them from picks, etc.

When the ditch is made a little too deep or when it is necessary to raise the tubes to get them over some obstruction, the filling should be done with earth and settled with heavy rammers. When blocking is resorted to, it must be of wood. Paving blocks or stones should never be used for this purpose. Especial care must always be taken to ram the soil well under tubes so that they may not ultimately depend on the blocking for support. It is also a good rule to let the line rest only on the packed dirt, and it should not in any case be allowed to rest solidly against any rigid body such as gas or water pipe.

Before the tubes are placed in the trench, the tinned ends of the copper rods should be well cleaned with No. 0 emery cloth, and any burs that may have been made in shipment should be carefully smoothed off with a file. The ends of the iron pipe must also be wiped clean. The tubes being laid in the trench, the coupling joint is then placed in position by first sliding it on to one copper rod and then slipping back on the opposite rod in the next tube, thus avoiding any unnecessary bending of the joints. The copper rods should project about $\frac{1}{16}''$ or $\frac{1}{8}''$ beyond the sockets of the coupling joints, and the soldering must be done very carefully with a regular soldering torch. Particular care must be taken not to burn or scorch the rubber plugs in the ends of the tubes. On the first application of heat, a *few drops* of soldering solution should be applied and great care must be taken that this is done *neatly* so that the solution does not run down the rod to the rubber plug. This is a very important point. Use as little soldering solution as possible and use it intelligently, where it will do the most good. When the joint is hot enough to make the solder run freely, it should be applied so as to run in between the joint and the rod, and all superfluous solder especially on the under side should be carefully wiped off while it is hot. When the soldering is finished, everything must be wiped up clean with a strip of cotton cloth. The ends of the rubber plugs should now be scraped to insure a clean dry surface, and after the joint has cooled off and has been inspected, it is ready to be inclosed in the box and insulated.

A pair of ball or cup clamps, as already described, are bolted on to the tubes at even distances from their ends, and the two halves of a coupling box are slipped over the clamps and bolted together, taking care to keep the flanges of the box level. The line should then be tested for insulation. If found all right the box is ready to be filled with the melted compound.

This compound should never be heated over 300° Fahrenheit, 200° to 250° being a good working temperature. It must be strained through a fine mesh strainer before pouring into coupling box. The box should be filled nearly to the top and when it has cooled, more melted compound should be poured in to fill up any depression caused by shrinkage and settling. After the second filling, the cast iron cap may be finally locked by giving it a quarter turn and this part of the line will be ready for the final operation of filling the trench and repaving the street.

Experience has shown that about nine-tenths of all faults in underground conductors originate at the joints. The cost of maintenance of an underground system will therefore depend largely on the character of the original work. It is important that none but strictly competent and conscientious workmen should be employed, and as an additional precaution all joints should be inspected before being covered up.

It is best to avoid putting in unnecessary services with the idea that they may be used at some future time. There are of course cases where it may be deemed expedient to do this, but as a general rule it will be found more advisable to put them in as they may be required. To facilitate this work, a map of the system should be made as it is laid, the joints being located with regard to fixed landmarks, so that when a new service is required, the exact location of the coupling box being known, only a small hole need be excavated.

The service pipe or cable should run into a dry basement or cellar, where this is possible. In every case the inside or house end must be properly protected from dampness and mechanical injury by means of End Boxes, as already described. Services should always be tested before being connected to main line.

In all work of this kind cleanliness and care are the most necessary factors to insure successful and economical operation.

JUNCTION BOXES.

It has already been stated that a feeder is a line that carries current from the central station switchboard to some center of distribution. Junction boxes are placed at these distributing points to facilitate the connection of the feeder to the different mains which branch out from it. In junction boxes all conductors of similar polarity are connected together, so that they may be considered as subsidiary bus-bars which not only receive and distribute current, but which also allow the transfer of current from one part of the system to another through the network of mains.

Junction boxes therefore serve, first, as centers of distribution, and secondly, as centers of equalization of electrical pressure between different portions of the system. They also afford a ready means of inspecting and testing any line, or of disconnecting a line from the system, when necessary.

JUNCTION BOXES FOR EDISON TUBE SYSTEMS.

Two types of junction boxes have been standardized for the Edison Tube System: Type 93 and Type 88. They are of cylindrical shape, and each box is provided with a strong and heavily ribbed outer cover to stand the wear and tear of street traffic, and a lighter inner cover which is bolted down against .a special form of rubber gasket, making a water-tight joint.   They are designed to be buried in the ground with the outer cover level with the street pavement.

TYPE 93 JUNCTION BOXES.

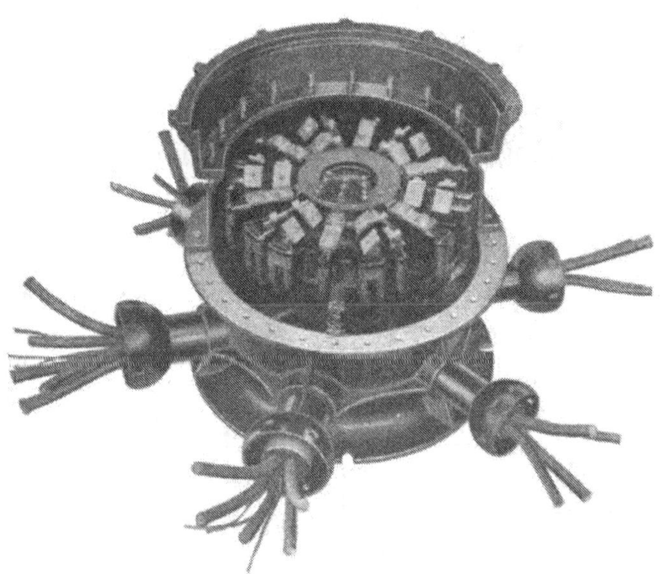

Fig. 19.

TYPE 93 JUNCTION BOX.

The Type 93 junction boxes are built to accommodate feeders up to 1500 amperes and mains up to 1000 amperes capacity, the fuse terminal contacts being 2″ x 2″.

They are built in three sizes for use with four, six and ten lines respectively.

The four-way box is generally used for the connection of mains at street intersections. It is furnished with four short projecting stubs for connecting to as many lines of main tubes.   It can, however, be furnished with one or more feeder stubs when required.

The six-way box has four stubs for connecting to mains, and two larger stubs for connecting to either mains or feeders.

The ten-way box has eight stubs for connecting to mains and two for connecting to either feeders or mains.

The feeder stubs in these boxes differ from main stubs only in having larger copper conductors with pressure wires.

Table of Dimensions and Weights.

Type 93 Junction Boxes.

TYPE 93 JUNCTION BOX.	NO. OF FEEDER STUBS.	NO. OF MAIN STUBS.	WEIGHT LBS.	DIMENSIONS IN INCHES.	
				Top Diam.	Height.
4 Tube Box	4	–	1850	$34\frac{1}{2}$	$30\frac{1}{2}$
4 " "	–	4	1150	$34\frac{1}{2}$	$30\frac{1}{2}$
6 " "	2	4	1850	$36\frac{1}{2}$	$30\frac{1}{2}$
10 " "	2	8	3850	$46\frac{1}{2}$	$30\frac{1}{2}$

These junction boxes are used for the following purposes :

First.   For the interconnection of tube mains.

Second.   For the connection of tube mains to tube feeders.

Third.   For the connection of tube mains to cable feeders, where the tube mains do not terminate in a manhole.

Fourth. For the interconnection of cable mains or tube mains and feeders in a "built-in" system without ducts.

TYPE 88 JUNCTION BOXES.

Type 88 junction boxes are similar in general construction to Type 93 boxes, but are intended for lighter service, being ordinarily built with fuse terminal contact $1'' \times 1''$ to accommodate feeders up to 500 amperes and mains up to 300 amperes capacity.

They are made in three standard sizes, each size having the same number of stubs as in the Type 93 box.

Fig. 20.

TYPE 88 JUNCTION BOX.

Table of Dimensions and Weights.

Type 88 Junction Boxes.

TYPE 88 JUNCTION BOX.	NO. OF FEEDER STUBS.	NO. OF MAIN STUBS.	WEIGHT LBS.	DIMENSIONS IN INCHES.	
				Top Diam.	Height.
4 Tube Box	1	3	500	$22\frac{3}{4}$	$30\frac{1}{2}$
6 " "	2	4	1000	$27\frac{1}{2}$	$30\frac{1}{2}$
10 " "	2	8	1500	$36\frac{1}{4}$	$30\frac{1}{2}$

When either the 88 or the 93 Type of junction box is to be used with *tube feeders* and mains, it is furnished with short stubs which can be connected to the tubes in the same way that tubes are connected to each other.

When *cable feeders* are used in place of tube feeders, the boxes are provided with a special feeder stub which is furnished with lead covered cable, so that standard cable joints can be made between the feeder proper and the cable in the box.

For systems that are composed entirely of cable laid directly in the ground, a junction box with special stuffing boxes is provided, so that the cable in the system can be run direct to the terminal inside the box, without any intermediate joint. Orders for boxes of this kind should specify the number of cables of each size which are to be accommodated in the box, and the over-all diameter of each size of cable, so that fittings may be bored with appropriate holes.

These junction boxes are fitted for the 3-wire, 220-volt system, but they can be arranged for the 3-wire, 440-volt system with grounded neutral, by the insertion of special contact rings and terminals with moulded arc-deflectors.

It sometimes happens that the street grading line is raised after a system of underground conductors has been installed, and it may then be difficult and expensive to bring up the entire junction box so that its cover would be at the new level. To meet cases of this kind, "extension rings" are made which can be set on the top of the junction box. These rings are made in three sizes for Type 93 and Type 88 junction boxes, being respectively $1\frac{1}{2}''$, $2''$ and $3''$ deep.

In locating junction boxes, the condition and route of street traffic should be considered, and they should be set in such positions as to interfere with the general travel as little as possible, when they are opened.

All parts of junction boxes are built to standard gauge and are interchangeable.

MANHOLE JUNCTION BOXES.

The best practice favors the use of Cable-feeders and Edison Tube mains, making a combination system, which embodies the best features of the "conduit" and the "built-in" systems, and adapts them to the various requirements of low tension transmission and distribution.

Fig. 21.
MANHOLE JUNCTION BOX.

A cable-feeder, being drawn through the conduit or duct, naturally terminates in a manhole. The tube mains are also made to project from 8 to 10 inches inside the manhole, and the ends are protected by "*end-boxes.*"

For the convenient interconnection of these various conductors, a line of so-called "Manhole Junction

Boxes " has been developed. They are rectangular in shape and are so arranged that they may hang against the wall of the manhole, or rest on the floor in any convenient position, but they are commonly supported against the wall.

Being used only inside the manhole and thus protected from the jar and pounding of street traffic, the containing boxes are made much thinner and lighter than those of Type 93 and Type 88 Junction Boxes.

The standard Manhole Junction Boxes are also perfectly adapted for use in connection with a system wherein cables are employed for both feeders and mains.

The accompanying illustration shows a standard Form E Three-wire Manhole Junction Box. These boxes are now built in four sizes, the four, six, eight and ten-way boxes having outlets respectively for twelve, eighteen, twenty-four and thirty cables, besides which each box is provided with one additional outlet for the pressure wires.

The positive and negative cables in these boxes may be of any size up to 1,000,000 c. m., and the contacts of the fuse terminals are 2″ x 2″, as in Type 93 junction boxes, so that similar fuses can be used in both types.

The neutral cables may be of any size up to 500,000 c. m. and the terminals are arranged for their direct connection to the neutral bus-bar, without fuses.

Standard plug porcelain cut-outs are provided for the protection of the pressure wires.

The positive, negative and neutral bus-bars are made of pure drawn copper of liberal cross section, and the arrangement is such that one-half of the cables of each polarity enter on each side of the box, thus avoiding the necessity of crossing the cables in the manhole and permitting them to be taken into the junction box with a minimum amount of bending.

The bus-bars and cable terminals are fitted with taper holes for the insertion of a flexible cable shunt around the fuse terminals, thus providing for the cleaning of the latter and the changing or renewal of fuses without any interruption of the service.

The minimum length of leakage surface on the insulating support is 2″, and all these boxes are tested with 5000 volts before shipment.

The cables enter the junction boxes through glands or stuffing boxes which make a waterproof joint between the cable and the box. The stuffing boxes are so constructed that they can be unscrewed from the junction box, leaving openings large enough to permit the insertion or withdrawal of the terminals. With this arrangement, all soldering can be done outside the box. As the stuffing boxes are interchangeable, the feeder may be brought from either side and attached to any part of the bus-bars, the better practice being to put it in the center.

Weights and Dimensions of
Form E Three-wire Manhole Junction Boxes.

SIZE.	NO. OF CABLES.	WEIGHT LBS.	OUTSIDE DIMENSIONS IN INCHES.		
			Length.	Width.	Depth.
Four-way	12	315	36	18	10
Six-way	18	415	50	18	10
Eight-way	24	500	62	18	10
Ten-way	30	600	74	18	10

If it is desired to have a wiped joint instead of a packed joint between the cable and the box, the removable pieces can be made with brass nozzles to which the lead sheathing of the cables can be united.

FORM A TWO-WIRE MANHOLE JUNCTION BOXES.

The practice of connecting neutral conductors on the so-called "Tree System" has been recently revived.

The method consists in running the neutrals independently of the positive and negative conductors and solidly connecting all neutral branches without safety fuses.

Many engineers now prefer this plan to the hitherto common practice of running the neutral wires everywhere parallel with the positive and negative wires and putting safety fuses at all neutral branch joints.

Weights and Dimensions of
Form A Two-wire Manhole Junction Boxes.

SIZE.	NO. OF CABLES.	WEIGHT LBS.	OUTSIDE DIMENSIONS IN INCHES.		
			Length.	Width.	Depth.
Four-way for Mains only . . .	8	87	16	$17\frac{1}{2}$	$5\frac{1}{2}$
Six-way for Mains only . . .	12	110	$20\frac{1}{2}$	$17\frac{1}{2}$	$5\frac{1}{2}$
Seven-way for Mains & Feeder	14	150	25	$17\frac{1}{2}$	8

The adoption of the neutral "Tree System" permits the use of smaller and cheaper junction boxes, as no neutral cables have to be accommodated, and on account of the limited space in manholes, the reduction in the size of junction boxes is frequently found to be desirable. To meet the requirements of this system, a line of Two-wire Manhole Junction Boxes has been designed, and three sizes, as shown in the preceding table, have so far been standardized.

Only the positive and negative conductors, and the pressure wires are taken into these boxes, the neutrals

Fig. 22.

FORM A TWO-WIRE MANHOLE JUNCTION BOX.

being connected solidly together in the manhole in any convenient way. If the neutral is purposely grounded, which is commonly the case, it is obviously unnecessary to insulate its ends in the manhole.

The accompanying illustration shows the Form A Two-wire Junction Box *for mains only*. Reference to the table will show that these boxes are made in two sizes for four and six mains respectively (8 and 12 cables.) The mains can be of any size up to 500,000 c. m. and the fuse connections are 1″ x 1″, taking the same size of safety fuses as the Type 88 Edison Junction Box.

A Form A Two-wire Junction Box for one feeder and six mains (14 cables, exclusive of pressure wires) is shown in the accompanying illustration. The twelve (12) main cables may be of any size up to 500,000 c. m. If, for instance, there should be only four mains, the four extra terminals may be very conveniently used for services. These boxes are designed for one two-con-

Fig. 23.

FORM A TWO-WIRE FEEDER BOX.

ductor concentric *feeder cable*, or two single conductor feeder cables of any size up to 1,000,000 c. m. and the necessary pressure wires.

Following the present standard practice of all large central stations, only the main terminals are fitted for safety fuses, the feeder terminals being bolted direct to the bus-bars. The feeder enters at the bottom of the box, and by disconnecting the feeder terminals from the bus-bars, and taking out four bolts which attach the nozzle through which the feeder enters the box, the feeder cable and terminal may be dropped down clear of everything for purposes of testing, etc.

The bus-bars that are used in these boxes are made of drawn copper and are mounted on supports of blue Vermont marble specially treated to prevent the absorption of moisture. A heavy barrier of the same material separates the positive and negative bus-bars.

The entire inner surface of the cover of this box is lined with specially treated asbestos, and every other portion of the box against which an electric arc might play, owing to the blowing of a fuse, etc., is protected by a covering of the same material.

Where paper insulated cables are used, this box can be arranged to be filled with oil after the cover has been bolted on, as there is nothing but metal, marble and asbestos in the box, and none of these materials can be injured by the oil. Boxes for the use of oil are provided with a valve at the bottom of the box through which the oil may be drawn off when it is desired to open it.

This type of box is simple, compact, durable, easy to install and of moderate price.

SURFACE JUNCTION BOXES.

For situations where the manholes are too small for the convenient installation of ordinary junction boxes, or where, owing to poor drainage and liability to frequent flooding, a box of this kind might not be readily accessible, the Surface Junction Box has been developed.

This box is made to fit around an eight inch pole, to which it forms an attractive base. It affords ample room for all the necessary fittings for any number of cables up to 20, together with a switch for an arc lamp on the pole, if one is used there. The box stands on the sidewalk, and is connected to the manhole by a curved iron pipe, as shown in Fig. 26.

Fig. 24.   Fig. 25.

SURFACE JUNCTION BOX

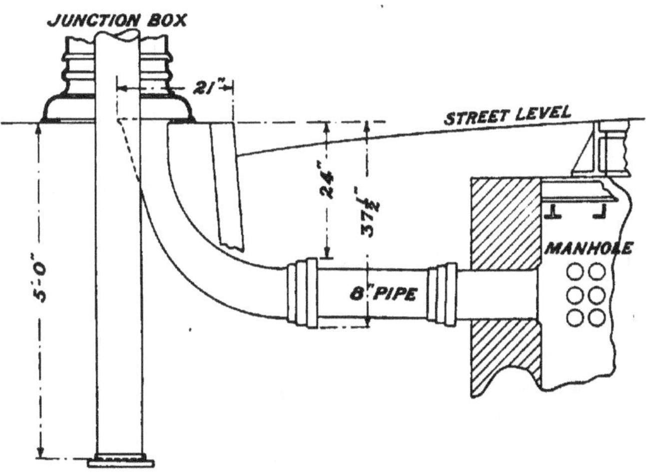

Fig. 26.

DIAGRAM OF CONNECTIONS OF SURFACE JUNCTION BOX.

SPECIAL JUNCTION BOXES.

The use of standard boxes is always extremely desirable, but in situations where they cannot be used, special boxes can be designed and constructed.

SERVICE BOXES.

When cable mains are used for the house to house distribution of electricity, it is often desirable to provide for the convenient connection and disconnection of services. Small subsidiary manholes or handholes, having cast iron covers level with the pavement, are frequently built in the line of conduit through which the main cables are drawn. They may be made of any convenient size, according to requirements, their depth being governed by the level of the conduit. When the cable main runs near to the surface, the openings may be smaller than when it is deeper down, owing to the increased difficulty of handling the cables at the lower level.

The cast iron service boxes placed in these subsidiary manholes or handholes are so designed that the positive, negative and neutral main conductors may run through them ·without being cut. After removing a small section of insulation from each of the three main

Fig. 27.
SERVICE BOX.

cables, the service wires are attached by suitable clamps and the box may then be filled with hot compound in the same manner as the Edison coupling boxes already described.

T and cross service boxes are made which are suitable for three-conductor mains and services, and also for mains and services that are composed of single conductor cables.

ELECTRICALLY OPERATED SWITCHES FOR UNDERGROUND LINES.

Electrically operated switches provide for connecting or disconnecting a distant line.

The switch manufactured by the General Electric Company has a maximum capacity of 1000 amperes at 250 volts, and is opened and closed by a ⅛ H. P. motor controlled by a small switch which may be placed on the station switchboard, or in any other convenient location. The heavy switch at the distant point is simple and positive. It is closed by a powerful toggle joint acting on connecting pieces of the laminated bridge type, so that no sticking can occur in opening. Supplementary carbon breaking pieces are also used to diminish the

Fig. 28.

ELECTRICALLY OPERATED SWITCH.

sparking at the terminals. The mechanism has only one worm and gear, and all the parts are readily accessible. The gear is mounted loose on the shaft and operates through a ratchet clutch which is released at the proper moment, thus permitting the motor to go on running without doing any harm.

Only one connecting wire is used between the small motor and the point of control, and as but little current is required, the neutral of the ordinary feeder pressure wires may be employed. The indications of the respective feeder volt indicators will necessarily be disturbed during the operation of the switching motor, but this momentary interruption in their service may be considered unimportant in comparison with the advantage of not having to install an extra wire. If, however, a spare pressure wire is available, it may be used to advantage.

Figure 28 is an interior view of a Form E electrically operated switch contained in a standard box, as designed for use in street manholes. These switches can also be fitted into round boxes like Type 88 or Type 93 junction boxes, for use in connection with an Edison tube system, or with any other built-in system of conductors.

They are not intended to break circuits under heavy load, but only to disconnect feeders or tie lines from the general system of conductors.

Electrically operated switches can be made in all sizes, and they are finding a wide field of useful application in the many new requirements of modern central station practice.

The weight of the switch illustrated in Fig. 28 is about 420 lbs. and its dimensions are as follows:

Length, 34 inches.
Width, 17 "
Depth, 12 "

CARRYING CAPACITY OF UNDERGROUND TUBING.

The "safe carrying capacity" of underground tubing is necessarily subject to a great amount of variation according to location and conditions, such as the change of temperature incidental to the different seasons of the year, and the nature of the soil in which the tubing is laid, etc. The capacity is also governed by the time limit of service, and in a broad sense by the comparative cost of maintenance.

It is therefore useless to formulate any *absolute* safe carrying capacity for the different sizes, and the most intelligent way to consider this problem is on the basis of a *safe temperature limit*, this being the governing factor of economical use and maintenance.

Experience has placed this limit at 45° C., so that taking the average temperature of the ground at a depth of two or three feet to be 15° C., a rise of 30° C. is allowable; but this temperature cannot be exceeded to any great extent without incurring risk of damage to tubing.

Assuming, therefore, an initial ground temperature of 15° C., also that the tubes are buried in ordinary moist earth, and that the ultimate temperature of the tubes shall not exceed 45° C. under conditions of continuous service, Table No. 1 gives the approximate safe carrying capacity as compiled from a large number of careful tests.

It is well known that in a three-wire system, the neutral conductor is only intended to provide for a temporary unbalanced condition of load, in which case, the current which normally flows in two conductors only, is split up among the positive, negative and neutral conductors. The resulting temperature, however, should not exceed the temperature caused by the same amount of current in the positive and negative conductors only.

In making the tests, therefore, from which table No. 1 was compiled, only two of the three conductors were used. These two conductors were connected to the source of electrical supply at one end and joined together at the other end, so that they formed a circuit within the tube.

The "maximum current" column in this table represents the current in this circuit, but as this current passes *twice* through the tube, the heating effect is equivalent to twice the actual current, as shown in the third column headed "Equivalent of Total Current in Tube."

The two conductors might be put in multiple and twice the "Max. C." (as given in second column) be passed through the tube in one direction with the same result in regard to temperature. If all three conductors, however, are connected in multiple, and three times the Max. C. (as given in the second column) is passed through the tube, or if the three conductors are connected in series and the Max. C. passed three times through the tube, the actual extra amount of heat generated in these cases would be 50% over that with load in two conductors only, but as the increase in heat produces a more rapid radiation and conduction from the surface of the iron tube, the resulting rise of temperature will be about 40%.

When, therefore, it becomes necessary to distribute current equally among all of the three conductors, the rating per conductor, as given in Table No. 1, must be reduced, although on account of the extra conductor brought into service and the consequent reduction in resistance per unit of length, the total capacity of the tube will be increased.

It must be remembered when estimating the carrying capacity of tubes that the individual capacities of the conductors enclosed will depend upon the manner in which they are to be used, and all calculations of capacity should be based on the watts lost per unit of superficial area of tube. The following is a general formula for comparing the current carrying capacities of tubes, when two and three conductors are loaded, respectively :—

$$\frac{3}{2} \times (\text{C. in 2 conductors})^2 = (\text{C. in 3 conductors})^2$$

Table No. 2, based on the above formula, shows the carrying capacity of the different sizes of tubes when all three conductors are of the same size, and are all equally loaded, the rise in temperature under conditions of continuous full load being the same as in Table No. 1.

Table No. 3 shows a comparison between the carrying capacities of tubes with two and three conductors loaded, respectively. It will be noted in this table that when all three conductors are used, the total carrying capacity of the tube is increased, although the individual capacity of each separate conductor is reduced.

As the heat developed in a conductor increases directly as the square of the current, a comparatively small increase of load beyond the rated capacity will produce a considerable increase in the temperature. It is therefore necessary to lay tubes with a broad margin of extra capacity in order that emergency overloads may be safely carried.

Table No. 1.

Showing Capacities With Two Conductors Loaded.
Main Tubes.

Size of Copper Rods.	Max. Current in Each of Two Conductors. 30° C. Rise. Amperes.	Equivalent Ampere Effect in Tubes. Amperes.
100	235	470
150	295	590
200	350	700
250	400	800
300	450	900
350	495	990
400	540	1080
450	580	1160
500	620	1240

Table No. 2.

Showing Capacities With Three Conductors Loaded.

Size of Conductors.	Max. Current in Each of Three Conductors. 30° C. Rise. Amperes.	Equivalent Ampere Effect in Tubes. Amperes.
100	192	576
150	240	720
200	285	855
250	326	978
350	404	1212
500	506	1518

Table No. 3.

Showing Comparison Between Carrying Capacities of Tubes With Two and With Three Conductors Loaded.

Size of Conductors.	MAX. CURRENT IN EACH CONDUCTOR. 30° C. RISE.		TOTAL CAPACITIES OF TUBES.	
	Two Wires Loaded. Amperes.	Three Wires Loaded. Amperes.	Equivalent Ampere Effect on Two Wires. Amperes.	Equivalent Ampere Effect on Three Wires. Amperes.
100	235	192	470	576
150	295	240	590	720
200	350	285	700	855
250	400	326	800	978
350	495	400	990	1212
500	620	506	1240	1518

CARRYING CAPACITY OF INSULATED CABLES.

In the following table, insulated cables are divided into two classes. When designed to carry a pressure not exceeding 2000 volts, they are called "Low Tension Cables"; but for any voltage above 2000 they are termed "High Tension Cables."

The tabulated figures are based on the use of single conductor low tension cables and triple conductor high tension cables, all cables being drawn into ducts and used under normal conditions. It is intended that the data here presented should be taken only as a guide for actual service, seeing that the safe carrying capacity of any cable will necessarily vary with changes in the surrounding local conditions, such as atmospheric temperature, proximity to steam heating pipes, etc.

A cable that is immersed in water will carry about 50% more current with a given rise of temperature than it will when run in a dry duct.

The effective radiating surface is evidently much less in conduits where a large number of ducts are built compactly together, than in cases where there are only a few ducts in parallel. It is, therefore, the safest practice to fix the allowable load on cables by a temperature limit, and experience has shown that the maximum temperature which cables should be permitted to attain is 60° C. for rubber, and 90° C. for paper insulation. At any higher temperatures there is great danger of permanent injury to the insulation, and all continuous working temperatures should be kept well below the above figures.

As paper will stand a higher temperature than rubber without deterioration, a paper insulated cable will carry more current than one of the same size insulated with rubber. This rule should, however, be applied only to *low tension cables* because the *puncture resistance* of paper and rubber decreases rapidly with increase of temperature, so that in cases where high tension current is used, it is not advisable to load a paper cable more heavily than a rubber cable, especially so, as with the same amount of current a paper cable will run about 10% hotter than a rubber cable, the insulation being of the same thickness in each case.

The table gives the maximum continuous load in amperes for high and low tension cables with rubber and paper insulation, the ultimate rise in temperature being marked at the head of each column.

Under ordinary conditions a cable will attain about 60% of its total rise in temperature during the first hour, 30% during the second hour, the final maximum being gradually reached during several following hours.

Concentric cables will safely carry about 20% less current on each conductor than the same size of single conductor cable.

Safe Current Carrying Capacity of Insulated Cables.

Size of Cable in Circular Mils.	LOW TENSION CABLE. SINGLE COND'R LEADED.		HIGH TENSION CABLE. 3 COND'R LEADED.
	Rubber Ins'n, 30° C. Rise. Amperes.	Paper Ins'n, 60° C. Rise. Amperes.	Rubber Ins'n, 30° C. Rise. Paper Ins'n, 35° C. Rise. Amperes on Each Conductor.
2,000,000	1670	2000	
1,500,000	1250	1600	
1,000,000	925	1200	
750,000	750	915	
500,000	550	660	440
400,000	460	560	360
300,000	370	450	290
250,000	320	390	250
200,000	270	310	210
150,000	220	260	175
125,000	180	210	140
100,000	160	190	125
80,000	140	165	110
60,000	110	130	85
40,000	75	90	60
No. 6 B & S Solid	50	60	40
No. 8 B & S Solid	30	36	24
No. 10 B & S Solid	20	24	16

TESTING OF INSULATED CABLES.

The large variety of insulated cables which the manufacturer is now called upon to produce involves many special tests. It may, however, be broadly stated that, in testing General Electric cables, the testing voltage is never less than double that which the cable is intended to stand in regular service, and the pressure test is maintained continuously on each cable for a period of at least one hour.

After the pressure test is finished, the insulation resistance is measured with a sensitive galvanometer and a battery current of 500 volts.

Conductivity tests are also made, and no copper is allowed to pass which does not show at least 98% of the conductivity of pure copper.

Capacity tests are likewise made whenever this factor may be of importance, as in alternating current work.

TESTING OF EDISON TUBES AND JUNCTION BOXES.

Before Edison Tubes are put into stock, they are subjected to rigorous tests as follows :

An alternating pressure of 5000 volts is maintained between each of the three copper rods for twenty minutes, a three-phase current being used for this purpose. The three rods are then connected together, and an alternating pressure of 5000 volts is maintained between them and the outside iron pipe for twenty minutes longer.

The insulation resistance between each conductor and the outside iron pipe is then measured with a sensitive galvanometer and a battery pressure of 500 volts.

The minimum of insulation resistance allowed is 3000 megohms per tube, the actual average insulation of each tube being from 27,000 to 40,000 megohms.

The conductivity of the copper rods is also tested and none are allowed to pass that do not show at least 98% of the conductivity of pure copper.

In the testing of junction boxes the terminals are all tested between each other, and between each terminal and the iron box with an alternating pressure of 5000 volts, the duration of each test being not less than one minute. The insulation resistance between terminals and between each terminal and the iron box is then measured with a battery pressure of 500 volts and a sensitive galvanometer, the minimum allowable resistance being 1000 megohms.

Should any weakness be discovered during these tests, the tube or junction box is returned to the factory.

From the foregoing brief outline of the usual testing process, it will be seen that no trouble is spared to detect defects.

ECONOMY OF THE THREE-WIRE SYSTEM.

The chief advantage of the three-wire compared with the two wire system, is the great saving of copper.

Representing the weight of copper in a two-wire system by unity, then in a three-wire system, distributing the same amount of current over a similar area, with the same amount of loss, the weight of copper would be $\frac{3}{8}$, or in other words, if a given installation on the two-wire system requires say, 80,000 pounds of copper, then by using the three-wire system, a saving of 50,000 pounds of copper would be effected, as the three-wire system would only require 30,000 pounds.

These figures apply to the distribution of current over mains, in which the neutral conductor is made equal in size to the outside conductors.

In the transmission of current by feeders, the economy is still greater, as it is usual to make the neutral wire of feeders only one-third the size of the out-

side conductors, thus reducing the ratio from $\frac{3}{8}$ to $\frac{7}{24}$, so that if 80,000 pounds of copper should be required in two-wire feeders, 23,330 pounds would effect the same results in three-wire feeders.

MULTIPLE-WIRE SYSTEMS IN GENERAL.

The saving in copper increases with the number of wires used in any multiple-wire system in accordance with the following simple formula, when the voltage between any two adjacent wires is practically the same in all the systems considered, or in other words, when incandescent lamps of the same voltage are used in each case.

Let n equal number of wires in system.

Then, Economy in Copper $= \dfrac{n}{2\,(n-1)^2}$.

Using the above formula, the copper required in a

2 wire system equals 1 or 100
3   "   "   " $\frac{3}{8}$ " 37.5%
4   "   "   " $\frac{2}{9}$ " 22.2%
5   "   "   " $\frac{5}{32}$ " 15.62%

A five-wire system was introduced in Germany some years ago, and a few plants were installed in this country, under this system. The troubles arising from its complexity, however, more than counterbalanced the saving in copper, and these installations have since been changed to the three-wire system, which seems to give the best combination of simplicity in construction with economy in copper.